DRAUGHTSMAN MECHANICAL SECOND YEAR MCQ

OBJECTIVE QUESTION ANSWERS

MANOJ DOLE

Copyright © Manoj Dole
All Rights Reserved.

This book has been published with all efforts taken to make the material error-free after the consent of the author. However, the author and the publisher do not assume and hereby disclaim any liability to any party for any loss, damage, or disruption caused by errors or omissions, whether such errors or omissions result from negligence, accident, or any other cause.

While every effort has been made to avoid any mistake or omission, this publication is being sold on the condition and understanding that neither the author nor the publishers or printers would be liable in any manner to any person by reason of any mistake or omission in this publication or for any action taken or omitted to be taken or advice rendered or accepted on the basis of this work. For any defect in printing or binding the publishers will be liable only to replace the defective copy by another copy of this work then available.

Digitization is the need of the time. In the future, training in industrial training institutes will need to be conducted using online internet to make training more convenient and easy. E-books containing a set of MCQ questions will be made available to the trainees as they need to be more accustomed to the multiple choice questions MCQ to prepare for the online exams taking place in their industrial training institutes.

With all these factors in mind, Mr. Manoj Madhukar Dole Instructor, Industrial Training Institute, Satara, has written books according to the new annual system and NSQF-5 syllabus. And they've created theoretical mobile apps and blogs to make training easier, and made all these educational materials available for download on the world famous websites Google Play Store, Amazon and Apple Book Store.

The books were published by Hon'ble Joint Director Shri Rajendra Ghume Saheb Regional Office of Vocational Education and Training, Pune on 9/1/2019, at this time Shri Prakash Saigavkar Saheb Principal Government Industrial Training Institute Aundh Pune, Shri Tukaram Misal Saheb Principal Govt. Q. Sanstha Satara, Shri Sachin Dhumal Saheb District Vocational Education and Training Officer Satara, Shri Yatin Pargaonkar Saheb Principal Govt. Q. Sanstha Kolhapur, Shri Vikas Teke Saheb Inspector Vocational Education and Training Regional Office Pune, Palekar Foods Products Pvt. Ltd. Entrepreneurial Chairman of Satara Mr. Nilkanthrao Palekar Saheb, Chairman of Hira Foods Mr. Ibrahim Baba Tamboli Saheb, Mrs. Shalmali Pawar Headmaster Government Technical School Center Satara and other dignitaries were present on the occasion.

Contents

Prologue

Draughtsman Mechanical Second Year MCQ is a simple e-Book for ITI Engineering Course Revised NSQF Syllabus, Draughtsman Mechanical Second Year. It contains objective questions with underlined & bold correct answers MCQ covering all topics including all about the latest & Important about skill in CAD application practical assignments are given by using commands in various methods. Detail and assembly drawing of machine parts viz., Pulleys, Pipe fittings, Gears and Cams applying range of cognitive and practical skills. Construct production drawing applying quality concept in CAD. Creation of objects in 3D Modeling Space and generate views, print preview to plot in .dwgand .pdf format. Individual skill is developed by preparing production drawing of machine parts applying conventional sign and symbol by taking measurement. Impart knowledge to draw workshop layout of a production industry considering process path and human ergonomics. In SolidWorks/AutoCAD Inventor/ 3D modeling environment the assignment is to create and plot assembly and detailed views of machine parts with dimensions, annotations, title block and bill of materials. and lots more.

We add new question answers with each new version. Please email us in case of any errors/omissions. This is arguably the largest and best e-Book for All engineering multiple choice questions and answers.

As a student you can use it for your exam prep. This e-Book is also useful for professors to refresh material.

Foreword

Vocational education and training is imparted through the Department of Vocational Education and Training through the Department of Business Education and Business Practical to supply multi-skilled artisans in line with the rapidly growing demand in the industrial sector in the 21st century. All the occupations within the institutions are important, as the trainees from these occupations develop multi-skills as per the demands of the industry.

with the noble intention of making available MCQ e-books suitable for all businesses, considering that all the examinations in all the industries in the industrial sector are conducted online and include MCQ method questions. Mr. Manoj Madhukar Dole has written a very good e-book on MCQ method as per the new annual syllabus. This e-book will definitely be a guide for all the trainees, trainee candidates, training instructors and others concerned.

The author of the book is Mr. Manoj Madhukar Dole, Instructor Gov. ITI Satara has 17 years of training experience. Written as a new annual pattern, this e-book incorporates modern digital QR Code technology to understand the layout, simple language, and simple syntax, diagrams and videos for each subject. So I am sure that this e-book will definitely be useful for in-depth study and exam practice. The work they have done is certainly commendable.

Mr. Tukaram Misal
Principal Government Industrial Training Institute Satara.

Preface

DGET New Delhi and CSTARI Kolkata have been implementing an annual pattern for all businesses in ITI since the August 2018 session. The examination system will also be changed and it will be online from this year and since all the questions are of Objective Type (MCQ), the trainees are in dire need of in-depth study. It is with this in mind that we are delighted to present the books based on the old NIMI pattern and a complete overview of the new annual pattern, and we hope that these books will be a guide for all business directors and trainees. Is.

For writing these books, Johar Awate Saheb, Principal of ITI Akluj. Former Principal of ITI Satara Saigavkar Saheb, Assistant Director Shri Chandrakant Dhekne Saheb Regional Office of Vocational Education and Training, Pune, District Vocational Education and Training Officer Sachin Dhumal Saheb and Headmaster Government Technical School Kendra Shalmali Pawar Madam and son Adhiraj Dole, mother Kusum Dole, I am very grateful to my father Madhukar Dole and wife Ashwini Dole for their special guidance and cooperation from time to time.

Also, in a very short period of time, the book was reviewed by Shri Rajendra Ghume Saheb, Joint Director, Vocational Education and Training Regional Office, Pune, for his invaluable time in publishing the book. I am sincerely grateful for their feedback.

I am grateful to the Instructor of ITI Satara for there continuous support from the very beginning of writing the book.

From this book, I consider myself blessed to have shared my thoughts on e-learning with you. I will not claim that this book is perfect, because considering the perfection, this book is an attempt and is in its infancy. They will be valuable for improvement if they are tested and suggested.

Manoj Dole
Dated 9/1/2019

Acknowledgements

The industrial training and theoretical examination system of our industrial training institutes and these changes have been accepted by the craft instructors and the trainees. Theoretical examinations conducted in your industrial training institutes are also conducted online. Since these examinations are of multiple choice MCQ method, the trainees will need to get more practice of such questions.

With all these considerations in mind, Mr. Manoj Madhukar, Director, Dole Crafts, Katari Industrial Training Institute, Satara, has done a thorough study and with his diligent work and added his keen intellect, according to the new annual system and NSQF-5 syllabus, e-book of Katari and other machine trades. -Book) and they have created mobile apps and blogs on theoretical topics to make training easier and have made all these educational materials available for download on the world famous websites Google Play Store, Amazon and Apple Book Store. Training has been made easier by creating a print version and using advanced techniques like QR Code.

All these educational materials will definitely be a guide for all the trainees for in-depth study and for the craft instructors and other concerned who are imparting vocational training.

CHAPTER ONE

Draughtsman Mechanical Second Year QR Code Images for e-Learning

Download App
Online Test Exam
ITI Books
AutoCAD CAM
JOB & Apprentice
Online Theory
Computer Course
Trading Course
CNC Course
MSCIT Course
Shopping Business
Internet Business
Web Designing
Online Services
Top Sportsmans
Indian Army
Freedom Fighters
Top Scientists
Social Reformers
Motivational Speaker
Top Richest People
Join WhatsApp Group
Join Facebook Group
Like Facebook Page
PAN / Adhar / Licence Passport

AutoCAD Command Shortcut Keys

CTRL+Q	Exit public consciousness
CTRL+R	Remove ornamentation
CTRL+S	Save as Stainless Steel
CTRL+SHFT+S	Save as a better design (ie. Titanium)
CTRL+T	Toggles Talent (requires administrative access)
CTRL+V	Value Engineer (reduces scale by 78%)
CTRL+SHFT+V	Pastes data from ArchRecord as Block
CTRL+X	Begin unpaid Furlough
CTRL+Y	Repeats last award winning design
CTRL+Z	Speed dial Zaha Hadid
CTRL+ZZZ	Sleep (not applicable)
CTRL+[	Cancels current schedule
CTRL+\	Cancels current budget
CTRL+ANGST+DEL	(no action)

F1	Displays Help wanted sign in café window
F2	Toggles all text to Helvetica
F3	Toggles Oh-SNAP
F4	Toggles MODERNISM
F5	Toggles ISOLATION
F6	Toggles CORBUSIER
F7	Toggles IRRELEVANT GRID
F8	Toggles ORTHO MODE (should always be on)
F9	Toggles POSTMODERNISM (should always be off)
F10	Toggles NORWAY
F11	Toggles ARROGANCE

AutoCAD Command Shortcut Keys

ALT+F8	Delete detail
ALT+F11	Add white
CTRL+1	Simplify Palette
CTRL+2	Remove Interior Design Palette
CTRL+3	Complicate Construction Process
CTRL+4	Add 4 extraneous sheets
CTRL+5	Remove Client's color Palette
CTRL+6	Remove Client's wife's color Palette (must press hard)
CTRL+7	Markup Set for interns (with only circles and question marks)
CTRL+A	Selects objects in drawing that aren't really needed
CTRL+B	Sends resume to B.I.G.
CTRL+SHIFT+B	Shifts blame to Consultants
CTRL+C	Copies angst to Clipboard
CTRL+SHFT+C	Copies angst to Clipboard with Base Point (ie. Finland)
CTRL+D	Delete relevance
CTRL+E	Cycles through design ideologies
CTRL+F	Flatten all roofs
CTRL+G	Insert 9-square Grid
CTRL+H	Insert Awesomeness
CTRL+L	Adds "Le" in front of all nouns
CTRL+K	Justify design concept
CTRL+L	Left justify design concept
CTRL+M	Less and/or more
CTRL+N	Insert new idea (bills client for additional time required)
CTRL+O	Opens ArchDaily.com
CTRL+P	Prints unemployment check

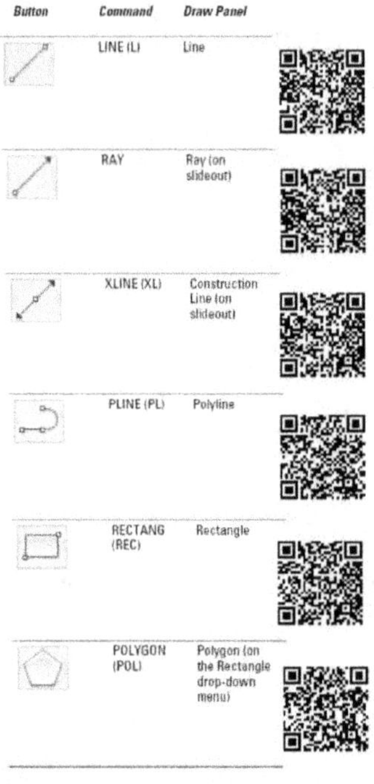

Button	Command	Draw Panel
	LINE (L)	Line
	RAY	Ray (on slideout)
	XLINE (XL)	Construction Line (on slideout)
	PLINE (PL)	Polyline
	RECTANG (REC)	Rectangle
	POLYGON (POL)	Polygon (on the Rectangle drop-down menu)

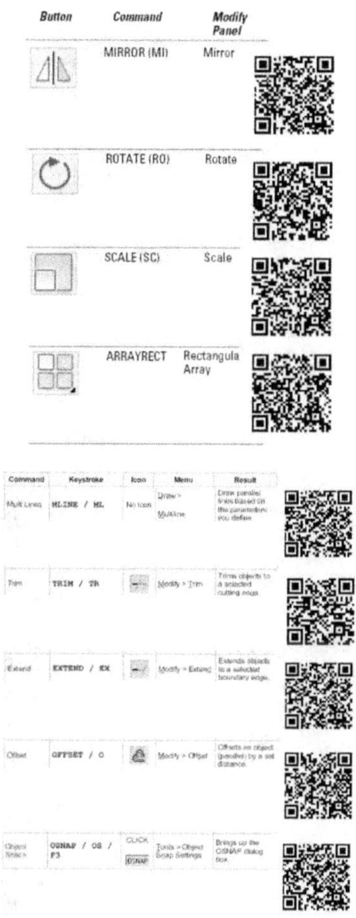

Button	Command	Modify Panel
	MIRROR (MI)	Mirror
	ROTATE (RO)	Rotate
	SCALE (SC)	Scale
	ARRAYRECT	Rectangular Array

Command	Keystroke	Icon	Menu	Result
Multi Lines	MLINE / ML	No Icon	Draw > Multiline	Draw parallel lines based on the parameters you define.
Trim	TRIM / TR		Modify > Trim	Trims objects to a selected cutting edge.
Extend	EXTEND / EX		Modify > Extend	Extends objects to a selected boundary edge.
Offset	OFFSET / O		Modify > Offset	Offsets an object (parallel) by a set distance.
Object Snap	OSNAP / OS / F3	CLICK OSNAP	Tools > Object Snap Settings	Brings up the OSNAP dialog box.

Icon	Command	Result
	EXTEND (EX)	Extend (on drop-down button)
	LENGTHEN (LEN)	Lengthen (on sidebar panel)
	BREAK (BR) two points	Break (on slideout panel)
	BREAK (BR) 1 point	Break at point (on slideout panel)
	EXPLODE (X)	Explode
	FILLET (F)	Fillet (on drop-down button)

Command	Keystroke	Icon	Menu	Result
Line	Line / L		Draw > Line	Draws a straight line segment from one point to the next
Circle	Circle / C		Draw > Circle > Center, Radius	Draws a circle based on a center point and radius
Erase	Erase / E		Modify > Erase	Erases an object.
Print	Print / Plot Ctrl+P		File > Print	Displays the Print/Plot Configuration Dialog Box
Undo	U (Don't use 'undo' for now)		Edit > Undo	Undoes the last command.
Rectangle	RECTANGLE / REC		Draw > Rectangle	Creates a rectangle after you enter one corner and then the second.

Button	Command	Modify Panel	
	ERASE (E)	Erase	
	MOVE (M)	Move	
	COPY (CO or CP)	Copy	
	STRETCH (S)	Stretch	
	ARRAYPOLAR	Polar Array	
	ARRAYPATH	Path Array	
	ARRAYEDIT	Edit Array (on slideout panel)	
	OFFSET (O)	Offset	
	TRIM (TR)	Trim (on drop-down button)	

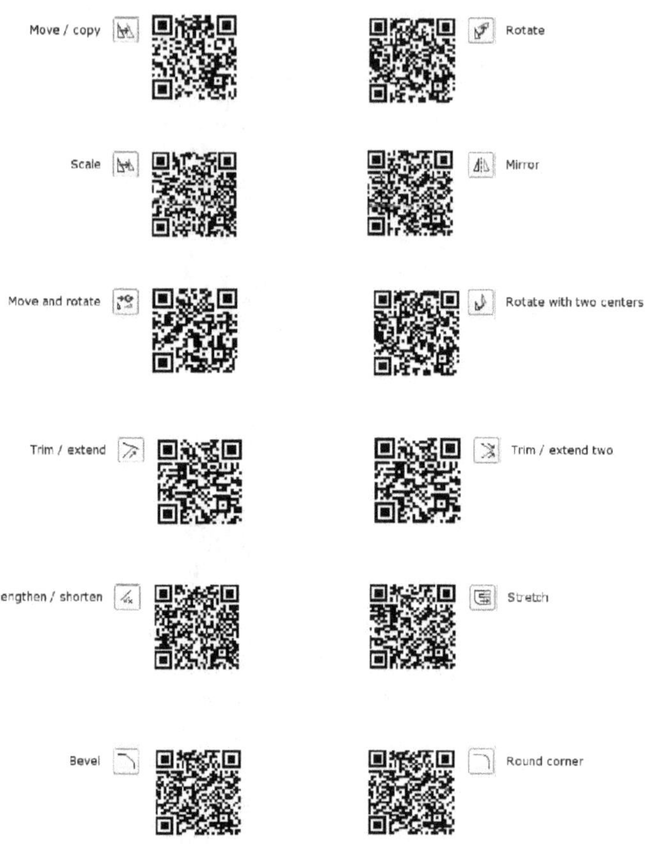

Move / copy
Rotate
Scale
Mirror
Move and rotate
Rotate with two centers
Trim / extend
Trim / extend two
Lengthen / shorten
Stretch
Bevel
Round corner

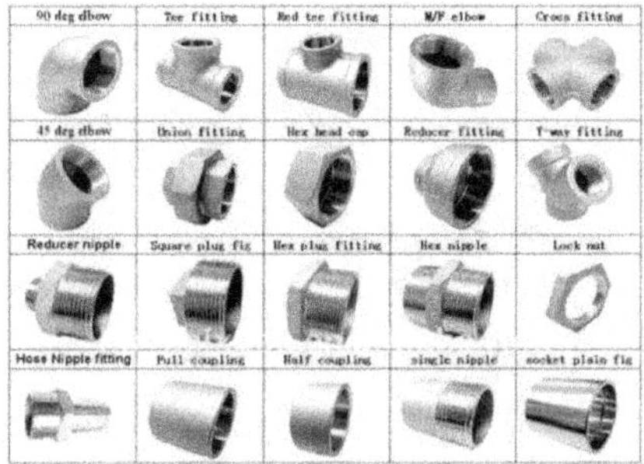

pipe joints

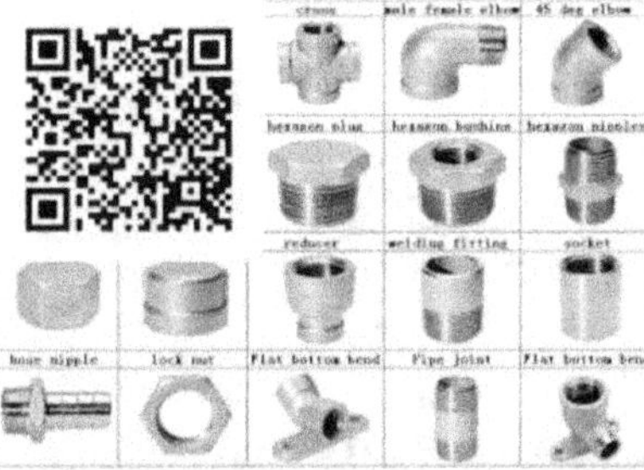

pipe joints

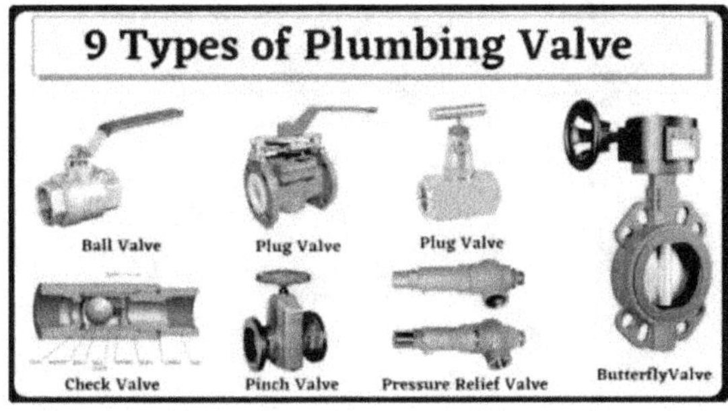

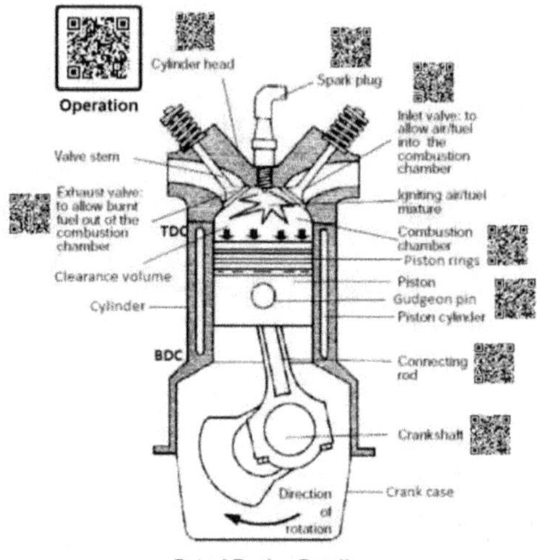

Petrol Engine Details

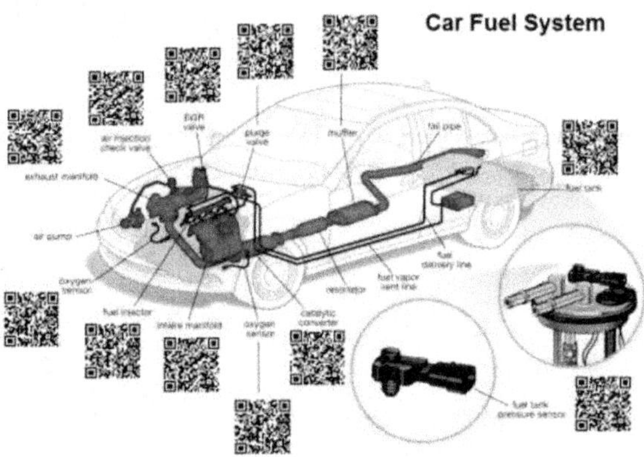

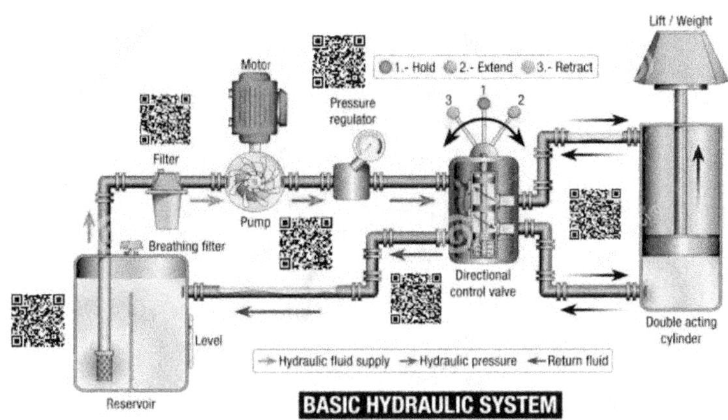
Lift / Weight
Motor
Pressure
regulator
1.- Hold   2.- Extend   3.- Retract
3   1   2
Filter
Pump
Breathing filter
Directional
control valve
Level
Double acting
cylinder
Reservoir
Hydraulic fluid supply   Hydraulic pressure   Return fluid
BASIC HYDRAULIC SYSTEM

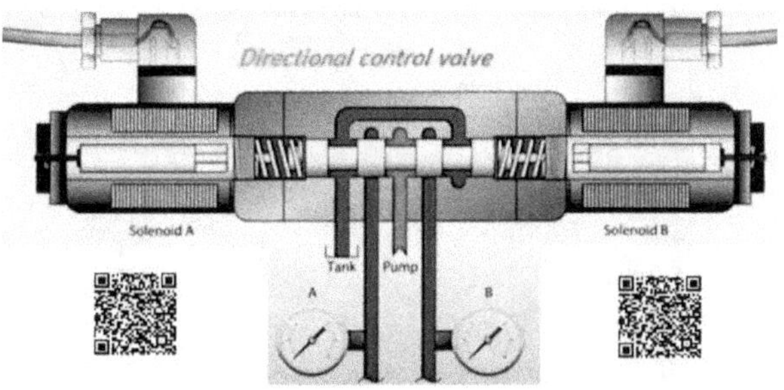
Directional control valve
Solenoid A
Solenoid B
Tank   Pump
A   B

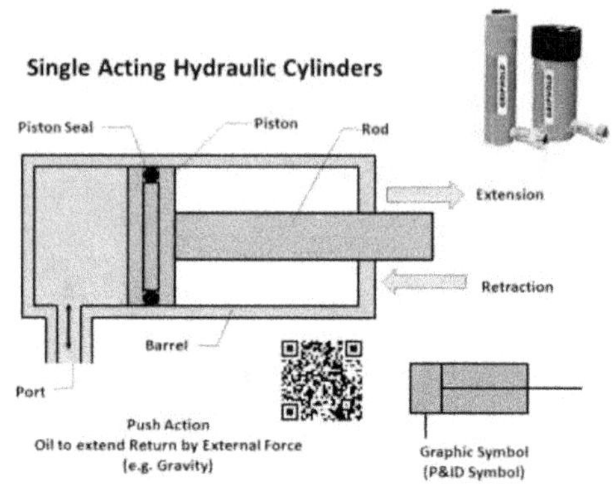

Double Acting, Single ended Cylinder

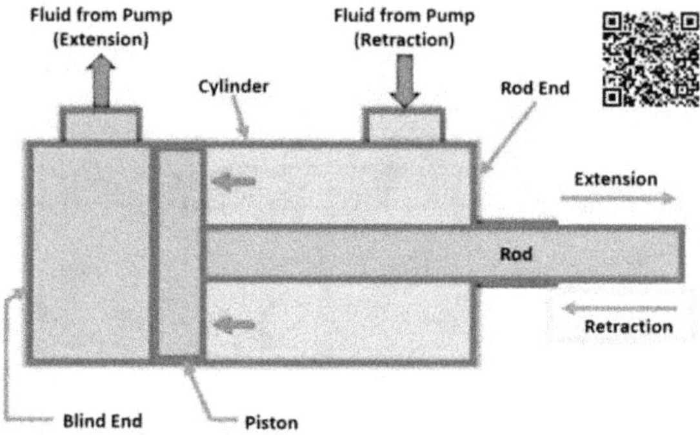

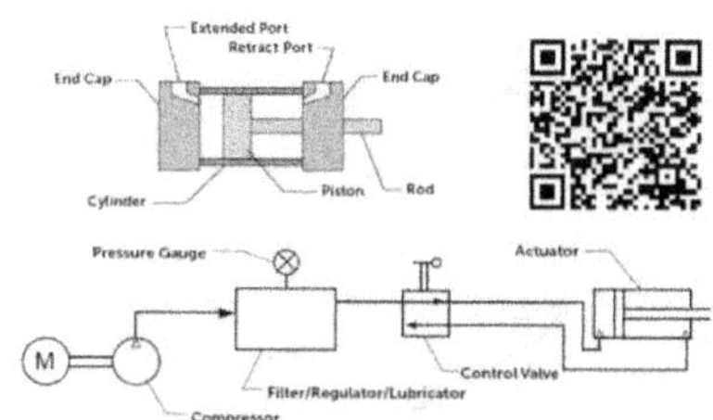

Pneumatic Cylinder System

Pneumatic directional valves

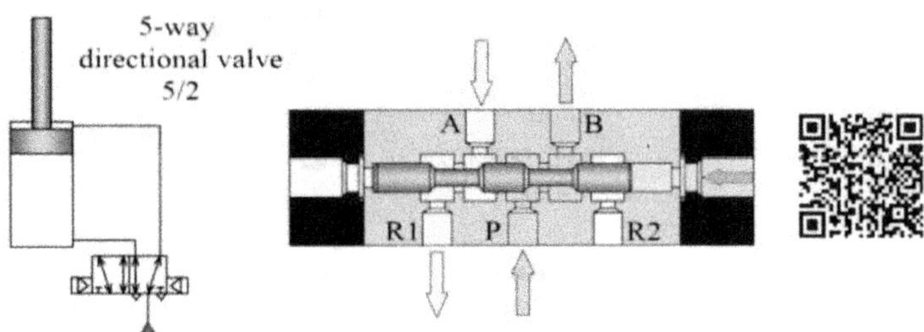

CHAPTER TWO

Draughtsman Mechanical Second Year MCQ

1] Which is the latest version of AutoCAD software?

a) 2016

b) 2017

c) <u>2018</u>

d) 2019

2] Which key is used to obtain properties palette in AutoCAD?

a) <u>Control+1</u>

b) Control+2

c) Control+3

d) Control+4

3] AutoCAD was first released in the year:

a) 1858

b) 1966

c) 1898

d) <u>1982</u>

4] How many units are available in AutoCAD?

a) 4

b) <u>5</u>

c) 7

d) 6

5] Which mode allows the user to draw 90° straight lines :

a) Osnap

b) <u>Ortho</u>

c) Linear

d) Polar tracking

6] To obtain parallel lines, concentric circles and parallel curves; __________ is used.

a) Array

b) Fillet

c) Copy

d) <u>Offset</u>

7] The default grid spacing in both X and Y directions is:

a) <u>10</u>

b) 20

c) 5

d) 15

8] How many workspaces are available in AutoCAD?

a) 2

b) 4

c) <u>3</u>

d) 5

9] Scale command can be accessed easily by typing:

a) SL

b) S

c) SC

d) <u>C</u>

10] Which command is used to divide the object into segments having predefined length?

a) Divide

b) Chamfer

c) Trim

d) <u>Measure</u>

447] How many grip points does a circle have?

a) <u>5</u>

b) 4

c) 3

d) 2

448] When drawing in 2D, what axis do you NOT work with?

A] X

B] Y

C] <u>Z</u>

D] WCS

449] The primary difference between the Model tab and the Layout tab(s) is ____.

A] the Model tab is used for drawing in 3D and a Layout is used for drawing in 2D

B] <u>the Model tab is where you create the drawing and a Layout tab represents the sheet that you will plot or print on</u>

C] the color of the background

D] the Model tab displays the drawing you are copying from and the Layout tab is where you lay out the new drawing

450] Which of the following is NOT a property of an object

A] Line weight

B] <u>Measure</u>

C] Hyperlink

D] Elevation

451] Which command convert discrete objects in polyline

A] Union

B] Subtract

C] Join

D] Polyline

452] To print the entire project, you will choose to regulate what to plot

A] Display

B] Extends

C] <u>Limits</u>

D] Window

453] What is the usefulness of viewports

A] <u>Allows us to see the screen or on paper different views of the same project</u>

B] Give us the ability to see projects have become a newer version of AutoCAD from our

C] We can make a change in one part of the plan, without affecting the rest

D] None of the above

454] What is the difference between the Scale command from the command Zoom

A] Scale for single object, while the Zoom whole plan

B] No difference

C] H Scale can grow / shrink a shape up 10 times, while the Zoom has no limits

D] <u>H Scale changes the size of objects, while the Zoom changes the visibility of the project</u>

455] When to fix a block attribute

A] <u>Before you fix the block</u>

B] When I make the block

C] After fix the block

D] No matter the number

456] What you cannot create from the command Offset

A] <u>Vertical straight</u>

B] Concentric circles

C] Three parallel lines

D] Parallel arcs

457] By what symbol shows the snap point to the closest point

A] with circles and dots in the center

B] With two triangle

C] <u>With three orthogonal</u>

D] With Diamond

458] Which state grid is use to design perspective

A] Parametric

B] <u>Isometric</u>

C] Pro-optic

D] Rectangular

459] If I want to draw a line in the direction 07:30 (local time) will give an angle

A] <u>-135 degrees</u>

B] 270 degrees

C] -225 degrees

D] None of the above

460] When in absolute Cartesian coordinates have points A (10.8) and B (6.5), then to make a line from A -> B with relative polar coordinates will write

A] @ -5 <36.88

B] @ 4 <30

C] <u>@ 5 <216,88</u>

D] @ 3 <60

461] What is the minimum allowable number of layers in a drawing

A] 0

B] 5

C] 1

D] 2

462] Which of the following is not a keyboard shortcut of AutoCAD?

A] Ctrl + P

B] Alt + F4

C] Ctrl + F4

D] Alt + B

463] Why do we have 16,7 M colors in RGB

A] Because so one can distinguish man

B] since this is the limit of graphics cards

C] For each color we have 256 shades and colors combination third

D] Because we want compatibility between PC and Macintosh

464] What setting gradient allows us to fill an open area?

A] Gap

B] Tolerance

C] Transparency

D] Open

465] What are the various options from left to right and the opposite direction?

A] Choose a different category of objects

B] select objects according to their color

C] Select objects according to their position

D] No difference

466] Which is corresponded to zoom mouse wheel?

A] Zoom in / zoom out

B] pan & scan

C] extents / all

D] scale

467] What command allows us to select objects based on some status?

A] Properties

B] Qselect

C] Pselect

D] Attributes

468] How to make a random line with an angle of 40 degrees to the x axis

A] will write 0 <40

B] will write 2 <40

C] will write 3<40

D] will write 4 <40

469] Which of the following file extensions cannot open the AutoCAD

A] dwg

B] dxf

C] <u>dot</u>

D] dws

470] A surveyor with a headband to measure the dimensions of a site, he make measurements by

A] <u>No one method</u>

B] Related Cartesian coordinates

C] Absolute polar coordinates

D] None of the above

471] What is the command used for Plagiostomi angle?

A] <u>Chamfer</u>

B] Fillet

C] Offset

D] Mirror

472] When should I use the Block Editor

A] To write text block

B] To fix outer block

C] <u>To fix dynamic block</u>

D] To store it in another version of AutoCAD

473] If the scheme that stores will be opened in AutoCAD 2006 then you must save it in

A] <u>AutoCAD 2004 dwg</u>

B] AutoCAD 2006 dwg

C] AutoCAD 2007 dwg

D] None of the above

474] Print scale 1:50 means that

A] The draft is 50 times less expensive than the original

B] <u>A 3 cm corresponds to half a meter</u>

C] A measure corresponds to 50 cm

D] None of the above

475] What do the letters UCS

A] Uniform Calculator System

B] United CAD System

C] Universal CAD Settings

D] <u>Universal Coordinate System</u>

476] What is the difference of two regular 8-gonon, which is one inscribed and another circumscribed circle
A] No difference
B] different opening angles
C] <u>different side length</u>
D] different crowd sides

477] If during the CCW measurement result gives an angle 135 degrees, the same CW angle measured is
A] 225 degrees
B] -135 degrees
C] -225 degrees
D] <u>135 degrees</u>

478] What does associative hatch
A] <u>Monitors the changes in shape that fills</u>
B] Relates to the other hatch plan
C] Both of the above
D] None of the above

479] What is the difference between command Plot and Print
A] plot command prints only big plans
B] The plot command for CNC (CAM)
C] <u>No difference</u>
D] print command can print up to A3 size paper

480] If you change the scale list a project that I have started from 1:50 1:10 then
A] You will have to start over
B] You should not raise the objects already exist (scale) by 5
C] You will not need to change anything in hitherto methodology
D] <u>should be converted into new items that will add based on the new scale</u>

481] Which of the following is NOT a unit of length measurement?
A] Yards
B] Parsecs

C] Microns

D] <u>Grads</u>

482] What does the command Wblock

A] Warp-speed block

B] <u>Write block</u>

C] Window block

D] Wide-area block

483] Where should you pay attention when you are working with autocad commands?

A] Drawing area

B] Status bar

C] Tool bars

D] <u>Command window</u>

484] Polar coordinates are used mostly for drawing______

A] Arc

B] Ellipse

C] <u>Angular lines</u>

D] None of the above

485] How many SNAP points does an object have?

A] 1

B] 4

C] 5

D] <u>Depend on object</u>

486] How many points do you need to define for the rectangle command?

A] One

B] <u>Two</u>

C] Three

D] Four

487] How many AutoCAD objects are in a rectangle?

A] <u>One</u>

B] Two

C] Three

D] Four

488] How will you deselect an object while you are selecting set of objects?

A] Ctrl+ click on the object to be removed

B] Shift + Click on the object to be removed

C] Alt + Click on the object to be removed

D] None of the above

489] How long will a line from 0,5 to 5,5 be __________

A] 10 units

B] 5 units

C] 15 units

D] None of the above

490] Objects are rotated around the

A] Bottom of the object

B] Base point

C] Center of the object

D] Origin

491] The origin of a drawing is at

A] 0,0

B] 1,0

C] 0,1

D] 1,1

492] How would you select set of objects in a drawing?

A] By a crossing window drawn from right to left

B] By a crossing window drawn left to right

C] Shift+ clicking on the objects

D] None of the above

493] Fillet command can be used to obtain__________

A] Sharp corners

B] Round corners

C] Both of the above

D] None of the above

494] A polar array creates new objects_____

A] In a grid pattern

B] In a circular pattern

C] In a straight line

D] All of the above

495] How many layers a drawing should have?

A] 1

B] 2

C] <u>As many as depending on the complexity</u>

D] None of the above

496] Scaling objects make them________

A] Smaller

B] Bigger

C] <u>Either smaller or bigger</u>

D] None of the above

1 Which command do you click for drawing line in Auto CAD

A Circle

B Line

C Arc

D Undo

Answer- B

2 From which menu bar do you get 'Line' command

A Layout

B Modify

C Draw

D Insert

Answer- C

4 Which option of command do you have to pick for creating a circle based on two end

points of the diameter

A 2P

B 3P

C TTR Centre

D Radius

Answer- A

5 Which keystroke do you type to use circle

command

A CO

B C

C O

D L

Answer- B

7 What do you mean by 'SER' in Arc command

A Start end radius

B Start end round

C Start easy radius

D Second end radius

Answer- A

10 Which menu bar has erase command in auto CAD

A Draw

B Modify

C Layer

D Setting

Answer- B

11 What is the keystroke for erase command in
auto CAD

A ER

B E

C ES

D EL

Answer- B

13 What is the shortcut key for 'undo'
command in auto CAD

A Ctrl + R

B Ctrl + Z

C Ctrl + V

D Ctrl + C

Answer- B

14 Which menu tab has undo command in
auto CAD

A Draw

B Modify

C Edit

D New

Answer- C

15 What is the alternative command of undo

A Redo

B Erase

C Delete

D Dot

Answer- A

16 From which menu tab do you find 'break'

command in Auto CAD

A Draw

B Edit

C Layer

D Modify

Answer- D

17 What is the keystroke for break command

A B

B BR

C BS

D EX

Answer- B

18 Why do we use 'Break' command in auto

CAD

A To erase the object

B to split the object into two parts

C To extend the object part

D To trim the selected part

Answer- B

2 In which toolbar do you find 'Move'

Command in Auto CAD

A Draw

B New

C Modify

D Edit

Answer- C

3 What is the keystroke for 'Copy' command

in AutoCAD

A CY

B CC

C C

D CO ''

Answer- D

4 What is the application of 'Copy' command in AutoCAD

A Multiplication of identical objects on the target points.

B Extend the object

C Move the object

D Repetition of command.

Answer- A

5 'Trim' command in AutoCAD is required for
_______ object

A Drawing

B Modifying

C Annotating

D Formatting

Answer- B

6 What is the shortcut key for 'Trim'
command

A TR

B TP

C TT

D TK

Answer- A

7 What is symbol of 'Trim' command in Auto
CAD

CAD " C 1

8 Which command do you use to draw
parallel line in specific distance

LINE OFFSET COPY MOVE

Answer- B

9 What is fillet command

A Rounding the sharp edge

B Cutting the sharp edge

C Break the corner edge

D Extend the edge

Answer- A

10 What is the shortcut key for 'Fillet' command

A C

B B

C F

D L

Answer- C

11 Which drop down menu contains 'Fillet' command

A Annotate

B Parametric

C Modify

D View

Answer- C

12 What is command prompt of 'Chamfer'

A F

B Cha

C Ex

D L

Answer- B

13 Why do you use 'Chamfer' command

A to bevel the sharp corner

B to break the line

C to radius the two corners

D to trim the two corners

Answer- A

15 What is command prompt of 'Rotate'

A RE

B RO

C R

D XR

Answer- B

16 What is shortcut command of 'Scale'

A SC

B A

C B

D S

Answer- A

17 Which command do you use for enlarging any drawing

A COPY

B SCALE

C ERASE

D ROTATE

Answer- B

18 Which command is represented by the given symbol

A Rectangle

B Offset

C Scale

D Copy

Answer- C

2 Which command prompt is used for insertblock

A J

B I

C L

D C

Answer- B

3 What is the basic use of I/Block for block

A For reusable contents

B For recreatingcontents

C For making object

D For editing contents

Answer- A

4 Which menu bar contains block command

A Insert

B Draw

C Modify

D Dimension

Answer- A

5 What is the shortcut key to make block command

A I

B B

C C

D L

Answer- B

6 Which command is used after making the required object to make block

A Mirror

B Block

C Copy

D Array

Answer- B

7 Which command panel contains 'Hatch' command

A Insert block

B Draw

C Layer

D Modify

Answer- B

8 What is the shortcut of 'Hatch' command

A B

B I

C H

D M

Answer- C

9 What is the use of 'Hatch' command

A To make multiple object

B To fill an enclosed area with a pattern

C To create new close object

D To split the object

Answer- B

11 In which command window do you find gradient

A Block

B Hatch

C Circle

D Array

Answer- B

13 What is the application of array command in Auto CAD

A Distributed copies of selected object in rectangular or circular pattern

B To create deflected object

C To copy object in irregular form

D To create scattered mirror image

A 2

14 How many types of array command are there in Auto CAD

A 3

B 2

C 1

D 4

Answer- C

15 What is polar array

A To make multiple copies of an object in circular pattern

B To draw any object in circular pattern

C To hatch any object

D To move any object

Answer- A

16 Which command panel contains array command

A Modify

B Draw

C Dimension

D Drafting Setting

Answer- A

17 What is main advantage of using array command

A It allows you to copy objects in a definite angle and exact no.of copy

B To enlarge the object

C To enclose the boundary of object

D To create mirror image of object

Answer- A

18 What is shortcut of array command

A A

B AR

C B

D C

Answer- B

1 What is a template in AutoCAD

A A file that is already setup for specific application

B A file contains different types of figure

C A command for creating identical object

D A command for making a block

Answer- A

2 A selected template file open in Auto CAD_________

A Model space

B Layout space

C Work space

D space

Answer- B

3 Which command is used for opening a template

A New

B Open

C Insert

D Format

Answer- A

4 Where do you click to create a new layer

A Layer properties

B Block

C Scale

D Circle

Answer- A

5 How do layers help

A Layer makes multiple objects

B Layer creates identical objects

C Layers allow to easy control and edit properties of a group of objects

D Layer makes block object

Answer- C

6 Which pull down menu contains layer

A Format

B Draw

C Annotation

D Help

Answer- A

7 What do you find in layer dialogue box among the followings

A Scale

B Line type

C Copy

D Displacement

Answer- B

8 Which sign should you click to disappear the layer from the screen in layer dialogue

box

A On freeze sign

B On bulb

C On lock sign

D On box sign

Answer- B

9 What is the shortcut command of layer

A LA

B L1

C L

D LO

Answer- A

10 What do you mean by 'DIMALINIER' command

A To draw a linear dimension

B To draw an aligned dimension

C To draw dimension for diameter circle

D To draw angular dimension

Answer- A

12 What is the command of dimension for radius for circles or arcs

A QLEADER

B DIMEDIT

C DIMRADIUS

D DIMDIAMETER

Answer- C

13 What command is used for doing own dimension style

A DIEMDIT

B DIMSTYLE

C DIM

D ANGULAR DIMRAIUS

Answer- B

16 Which one of these options pallate is found in Modify Dimension Style dialogue box

A Primary units

B Polar tracking

C By layer

D Format

Answer- A

17 What will be the command prompt to create new dimension style

A DDIM

B DIMEDIT

C QLEADER

D DIM RADIUS

Answer- A

1 What do you mean by 3D

A Four dimension

B Three dimension

C Two dimension

D One dimension

Answer- B

2 What is the advantage of 3D

A Helps to reduce size in design

B Helps you conceptualize design

C Helps to edit work in design

D Helps to print the drawing

Answer- B

3 Which toolbar do you click on Auto CAD window for 3D drawing environment

A Draw

B Modify

C Workspace

D Format

Answer- C

4 Which command panel / ribbon contains 3D primitives in 3D modelling drawing space

A Home

B Solid

C Insert

D View

Answer- B

6 Which one is 3D primitive command among these options

A LINE

B POLYGON

C CIRCLE

D CONE

Answer- D

7 What is the shortcut of Extrude command

A EX

B E

C Ext

D ED

Answer- C

8 In Which direction height of extrusion is measured

A X Direction

B Y Direction

C Z Direction

D XZ Direction

Answer- C

9 What is the shortcut of revolve command

A R

B RE

C REV

D REC

Answer- C

10 Why does the revolve command is used
A To create a solid model
B To create 2D object
C To rotate object
D to move object
Answer- A
11 What is the full form of UCS
Universal Coordinate system
Use co-ordinate system
Usual co-ordinate system
Union co-ordinate system
Answer- B
12 Default origin of UCS is
A World
B Current
C Universal
D Local
Answer- A
13 In which command panel do you find 3D rotate
A Modify
B Draw
C Format
D Insert
Answer- A
14 What is the use 3D rotate command
A Helps to rotate 3D object
B Helps to copy 3D object
C Helps to pull 3D object
D Helps to align 3D object
Answer- A
15 Which ribbon is combined with plot command in Auto CAD window
A Home
B Output
C Layout
D View
Answer- B
16 What is shortcut of print command
A Ctrl + X

B Ctrl + C

C Ctrl + P

D Ctrl + F

Answer- C

17 What is full preview

A Preview the print after plot setting

B Preview of parts drawing

C Properly drawing object

D Perfectly print drawing

Answer- A

18 Which command dialogue box contains preview command

A Plot

B Drafting setting

C Drawing units

D Plotter manager

Answer- A

1 Which one of the following drives is used for transmitting power without slip

A Belt drive

B Chain Drive

C Rope drive

D Jokey pulley

Answer- B

2 Which of the following is used for chain drive

A Spur gear

B Idler gear

C Sprockets

D Worm gear

Answer- C

3 What will be the diameter of cotton rope

5 mm to 10 mm

70 mm to 80 mm

25 mm to 50 mm 10 mm to 20 mm

Answer- C

4 What is the another name of speed cone pulley

A Built up pulley

B Stepped pulley

C C.I pulley

D V belt pulley

Answer- B

5 Whys the crowning of pulley done

A To make than more stylish

B To avoid slipping of the belt

C To make pulley more pleasant

D To make pulley light weight

Answer- B

6 What is material of Pulley

A CI

B Plastic

C Lather

D Fabric

Answer- A

7 What is the effect of 'V' groove on the pulley

A No friction grip of 'V' belt

B To increase friction grip of 'V' belt

C to decrease friction grip of 'V' belt

D Less friction grip of 'V' belt

Answer- B

8 What is material of 'V' belt

A CI

B Fabric & Rubber

C Cotton

D Steel

Answer- B

9 What is the including angle of 'V' belt

A 15°

B 30°

C 40°

D 60°

Answer- C

10 What is the angle of arc of contact with pulley of equal dia

A 120°

B 180°

C 45°

D 30°

Answer- B

11 What will be the factor on which power transmission by a belt depends

A Centre distance between the two pulleys on which belt passing

B Depend on width of belt

C Diameter of pulley

D Slip of belt

Answer- A

12 What will be the velocity ratio equals to N2 / N1 in a belt drive

A d2 / d1

B d2 / r1

C d1 / d2

D r2 / d1

Answer- C

13 What is known as the upper side in a belt drive having less tension

A Slack side

B tight side

C Driving distance

D Slip of belt

Answer- A

14 The Jockey pulley is fitted on the belt for...

A increase the arc of contact

B decrease the wrapping angle

C increase the rpm

D decrease the belt tension

Answer- A

15 How many basic types are in pulleys

A 2

B 3

C 4

D 5

Answer- D

16 What is the use of open belt drive

A to rotate the driven pulley in same direction of driving pulley

B To rotate the driven pulley in opposite direction of driving pulley

C To get different velocity

D To maintain the maximum speed

Answer- A

17 How many methods of mounting a pulley rigidly on a shaft

A 2

B 3

C 4

D 5

Answer- B

18 Due to localised movement of the belt resulting elastic stretch which is known as...

A slip

B creep

C crown

D lap

Answer- B

1 Which type of pipe is corrosion resistant and more flexible

A W.I. pipe

B C.I. pipe

C Plastic pipe

D Steel pipe

Answer- C

2 Which kind of pipe used for high pressure or high temperature

A Steel pipe

B Wrought iron pipe

C Plastic pipe

D Lead pipe

Answer- A

3 Which kind of pipe is generally used for domestic purpose where pipe line contains frequent bent.

A Cast iron pipe

B Wrought iron pipe

C Steel pipe

D PVC pipe

Answer- D

4 What is the thread angle of pipe thread

A 55°

B 60°

C 47°

D 29°

Answer- A

5 Which process is used to join copper & brass tubes

A Welding
B Brazing or soldering
C Couplings
D Spigot and socket joint
Answer- B
6 Which kind of iron is used for manufacturing of CI pipes
A White cast iron
B Grey cast iron
C Ductile cast iron
D Wrought iron
Answer- B
7 Which fitting is used to increase the length of pipe
A Socket
B Plug
C Nipple
D Cross
Answer- A
8 Where the elbow fitting used
A At cross
B At an angle
C At straight line
D Used for reducing diameter
Answer- B
9 Which type of pipe fitting is used for reducing diameter of pipe
A Nipple
B Reducer
C coupler
D Tee
Answer- B
10 Why is the plug used in pipe fittings
A To change length of pipe
B To close a pipe at end
C To join at 900
D To reduce the dia of pipe
Answer- B
11 Which is the standard metal bend fitting to change the direction of pipe
A 180°

B 360°

C 90°

D 40°

Answer- A

12 Which type of pipe fitting is used to connect a

A branch pipe

B Plug Tee

C Elbow

D Socket

Answer- B

13 What is the material of PVC pipe

A Steel

B Plastic

C Copper

D Clay

Answer- B

14 Which type of pipe is commonly used for water , steam , oil and gas

A Copper or PVC

B Steel or wrought iron pipe

C Steel or PVC

D Wrought iron or copper

Answer- B

16 Where will you se union or flanged union joint

A Fluids carried under high pressure

B For easy maintenance

C Connecting cast iron pipes

D Connect large diameter pipe

Answer- B

17 Which pipe joints are used to connect the large diameter pipes

A Flange joints

B Spigot and socket joints

C Hydraulic pipe joints

D Union joints

Answer- A

18 Which kind of pipe joints are used for carrying fluids under high pressure

A Expansion joint

B Hydraulic pipe joint

C Socket & spigot joint

D Flange joints

Answer- B

1 What is called the number of gears connected together

A Gear system

B Gear train

C Gear line

D Gear network

Answer- B

2 What is the full form of PCD in gear

A Pitch circle depth

B Pitch circle diameter

C Pick circle dia

D Circular diameter

Answer- B

3 How many types of gear teeth profile are generally used

A 2

B 3

C 4

D 5

Answer- A

4 Which is called the diameter at the bottom of the tooth spaces

A Pitch circle diameter

B Root diameter

C Crest circle diameter

D Addendum circle diameter

Answer- B

5 What is called the smaller one in pair of gears

A Gear

B Rack

C Pinion

D Spur gear

Answer- C

6 Which type of gear is used while two intersecting and co-planer shafts are connected by gears

Helical gear

Spur gear

Bevel gear

Spiral gear

Answer- C

7 Which gear is used to transmit power in two parallel shafts with axial thrust

A Helical gear

B Bevel gear

C Spur gear

D Spiral gear

Answer- A

8 What is the definition of DP in gear

A Ratio of number of teeth to PCD

B Ratio of PCD to number of teeth

C Ratio of CP to PCD

D Ratio of CP to number of teeth

Answer- A

11 What is the sum of addendum and dedendum called

A Working depth

B Spall width

C Whole depth

D Clearance

Answer- C

12 What is the included angle of double helical gear

A 900

B 450

C 1200

D 600

Answer- C

13 What type of gears are used to convert rotating motion into linear motion

A Rack and pinion gear

B Bevel gears

C Spur gears

D Helical gears

Answer- A

15 What type of gear is needed to transmit motion between two parallel shaft

A Bevel gear

B Spur gear

C Rack

D Worm gear

Answer- B

16 What is the example of non intersecting and perpendicular axes gear transmission

A Spure gear

B Worm and worm wheel

C Bevel gear

D Helical gear

Answer- B

17 What is gear train called if the axis of first and last gear are co-axial

A Simple gear train

B Compound gear train

C Reverted gear train

D Epicylic gear train -

Answer- C

18 Which gear profile has the infinite pitch radius

A Bevel gear

B Spur gear

C Rack

D Worm gear

Answer- C

19 Which one of the following is proportion of

simple indexing of gear cutting

A 10/N

B 20/N

C 30/N

D 40/N

Answer- D

20 Which one of the following drive is used for transmitting power with out slip

A Belt drive

B Gear drive

C Rope drive

D Pulley drive

Answer- B

22 What is the most common type of gear used

A Bevel gear

B Spur gear

C Helical gear

D Worm gear

Answer- B

23 What do you understand by DP

A Drill angle

B Diametral Pitch

C Dial pitch

D Circular pitch

Answer- B

24 What is the other name of double helical gear

A Spur gear

B Bevel gear

C Herringbone gear

D Metre gear

Answer- C

25 Which gear is used for high speed and heavy duty

A Helical gear

B Spur gear

C Bevel gear

D Rack

A

27 What is the pressure angle of spur gear tooth

A 14 ½°

B 22°

C 25°

D 28°

Answer- A

28 Which type of gear is used to change the shaft direction

A Spur gear

B Bevel gear

C Helical gear

D Worm gear

Answer- B

1 Which kind of cam is needed for reciprocating motion of follower

A Tangent cam

B Circular cam

C Cylindrical cam

D Edge Cam

Answer- D

2 Which factor effects the size of a cam

A Basic circle

B Hub size

C Pressure Angle

D Prime circle

Answer- C

3 How many types of radial cam are there

A 2

B 3

C 4

D 5

Answer- B

4 How many types of cam are there according to motion

A 2

B 3

C 4

D 5

Answer- A

5 How many types of cams are there according to shape and application

A 2

B 3

C 4

D 5

Answer- C

6 What is the other name of disk cam

A Grooved cam

B Plate cam

C End cam

D Cylindrical cam

Answer- B

7 Which mechanism is needed for auto motion

A Gear mechanism

B Cam mechanism

C Pulley mechanism

D Belt mechanism

Answer- B

8 Which kind of motion as given by tangent cam to follower

A Oscillating motion

B Linear motion

C Vertical motion

D Circular motion

Answer- A

9 Which type of motion of follower is best for high speed cam

A SHM follower motion

B Uniform acceleration and retardation of follower motion

C Cycloidal motion

D Linear motion

Answer- C

10 Which is the type of motion of a pendulum in a clock

A Oscillating motion

B Linear motion

C Rotary motion

D Reciprocating motion

Answer- A

11 What will be the type of angle when the follower begins to rise till it reaches its

highest position by moving the cam

A Angle of Ascent

B Angle of Dwell

C Angle of Descent

D Angle of action

Answer- A

13 What is the name of the angle moved by the cam from beginning of ascent to the

termination of descent

A Angle of action

B Angle of ascent

C Angle of Dwell

D Angle of descent

Answer- A

14 What is the name of smallest circle drawn to the cam profile from the cam centre

A Prime circle

B Base Circle

C Pitch circle

D Pitch curve

Answer- B

15 What is the smallest circle that can be drawn from the centre of cam and tangent to the

pitch curve

A Base circle

B Pitch circle

C Prime circle

D Pitch curve

Answer- C

16 How many types of follower are there

A 2

B 3

C 4

D 5

Answer- C

17 In which type of follower sliding motion takes place

A Knife edge follower

B Roller follower

C Flat traced follower

D Spherical faced follower

Answer- A

1 What is eccentric Special form of a crank mounted on crank shaft

A Type of D

B Slide value

C Type of piston

D Type of connecting rod (eccentric)

Answer- A

3 What is the use of eccentric

A To provide a short reciprocating motion

B To alternate compression and tensile stress

C To enable piston rod and valve rod to pass through cylinder end

D To provide movable cover (eccentric)

Answer- A

4 What is the purpose of piston ring

A To control combustion pressure

B To control wear and tear

C To control temperature

D To control air fuel ratio

Answer- A

5 What is material of piston ring

A Brass

B Copper

C Cast iron

D Aluminium

Answer- C

6 Which part of the piston is subjected to high pressure and temperature

A Crown

B Skirt

C Land

D Ring section

Answer- A

7 Which of the following is used to connect the connecting rod and other end of the piston rod

A Piston rod

B Cross - head

C crank shaft

D Eccentric

Answer- B

8 What is the another name of cross head

A Guide block

B Piston

C Crank shaft

D Stuffing box

Answer- A

9 What is the function of cross head

A To transmit motion

B To transmit thrust due to obliquity of connecting rod to bars

C To connect stuffing box

D To convert reciprocating motion to rotary motion

Answer- B 2

10 What is steam engine

A External combustion

B Internal combustion

C Two stroke engine

D Four stoke engine

Answer- A

11 Which part of steam engine prevents the leakage of fluid along the sliding rod

A Piston

B Connecting rod

C Stuffing box

D Cross - head

Answer- C

12 Which part of steam engine connect the piston rod with connecting rod

A Stuffing box

B Eccentric

C Cylinder cover

D Cross - head

Answer- D

13 Which part of the steam engine converts rotary motion of the crank into linear motion of the D - slide value

A Eccentric

B Connecting rod

C Stuffing box

D Piston rod

Answer- A

14 Which device is used for increasing the pressure of feed water

A Injector

B Feed pump

C Feed check value

D Blow off cock

Answer- B

15 Which part is fitted to the rear end of the crank shaft

A Piston

B Fly wheel

C Valve

D Cross - head

Answer- B

16 Which part of engine is used as storage of rotational energy

A Fly wheel

B Crank shaft

C Cross-head

D Stuffing box

Answer- A

17 What is the material of connecting rod

A Mild steel

B Aluminium

C Alloy steel

D Cast iron

Answer- C

18 Which part is connected by crank shaft and connecting rod

A Cylinder head

B Cylinder block

C Piston

D Cam shaft

Answer- C 1

19 What is the function of connecting rod

A To provide a tight fitting joint between two surfaces

B Transmits power from the piston to the crank shaft

C To connect thepiston to connecting rod

D To support the crank shaft

Answer- B

20 What is the advantage of two stroke IC engine

A Low power to weight ratio

B More moving parts

C More torque even at idling speed

D More no of strokes per cycle

Answer- C

22 What is called by the distance between BDC and TDC

A Bore

B Stroke

C Cycle

D Compression ratio

Answer- B

23 Which part of the engine sucks diesel from diesel tank

A Fuel injection pump

B Fuel filters

C Fuel injector

D fuel feed pump

Answer- D

24 What is the function of a fuel injector

A Draw diesel from the tank

B To clean the fuel

C To inject the fuel in the cylinder

D To connect piston with crank shaft

Answer- C

25 Which parts is uscd to form air and petrol mixture in petrol engine

A Spark plug

B Carburetor

C Fuel feed pump

D Fuel injection pump

Answer- B

28 What is the ratio of B.H.P and IHP called

A Volumetricefficiency

B Thermal efficiency

C Engine capacity

D Mechanical efficiency

Answer- D

137] Which type of component is used in hydraulic power unit?

A] Pressure gauge

B] filler gauge

C] valve

D] reservoir

138] Which type valve that lets air into the reservoir of a compressor , but does not let it out?

A] check valve

B] receiver valve

C] control valve

D] Three way valve

139] Which type valve restricts air flow?

A] shuttle valve

B] direction control valve

C] single acting cylinder

D] throttle valve

140] which part convert fluid flow into mechanical movement in a hydraulic system?

A] strainers

B] <u>actuator</u>

C] accumulator

D] pump

141] What is the name of component responsible for keeping the oil free of solids contamination?

A] Pumps

B] accumulator

C] <u>strainers & filters</u>

D] valves

142] What is the name of heart of hydraulic system?

A] valves

B] <u>pump</u>

C] accumulator

D] oil tank

143] Which type hydraulic cylinder is used the fluid acts on both sides of the piston?

A] Duplex cylinder

B] <u>double acting cylinder</u>

C] single acting cylinder

D] pneumatic cylinder

181] A pneumatic symbol is:

a) <u>Different from a hydraulic symbol used for the same function</u>

b) The same as a hydraulic symbol used for the same function

c) Not to be compared to a hydraulic symbol used for the same function

d) None of the mentioned

182] Pneumatic systems usually do not exceed:

a) <u>1 hp</u>

b) 1 to 2 hp

c) 2 to 3 hp

d) 4 to 5 hp

183] Most hydraulic circuits:

a) <u>Operate from a central hydraulic power unit</u>

b) Use air-over-oil power units

c) Have a dedicated power unit

d) Does not have dedicated power unit

184] Hydraulic and pneumatic circuits:

a) Perform the same way for all functions

b) Perform differently for all functions

c) <u>Perform the same with some exceptions</u>

d) Does not perform all the functions

185] The lubricator in a pneumatic circuit is the:

a) First element in line

b) Second element in line

c) <u>Last element in line</u>

d) Third element in line

186] When comparing first cost of hydraulic systems to pneumatic systems, generally they are:

a) More expensive to purchase

b) <u>Less expensive to purchase</u>

c) Cost is same

d) Cost is not required

187] When comparing operating cost of hydraulic systems to pneumatic systems, generally they are.

a) More expensive to operate

b) <u>Less expensive to operate</u>

c) Cost is same to operate

d) Cost is not required

188] The most common hydraulic fluid is:

a) Mineral oil

b) Synthetic fluid

c) <u>Water</u>

d) Gel

189) Which fluid is used in hydraulic power systems?

a] water

b] oil

c] non-compressible fluid

d] <u>all of the above</u>

190) Pressure of 1 bar is equal to

a] <u>14]5 psi</u>

b] 145 psi

c] 12]5 psi

d] 145 x 10-6 psi

191) What effect does overloading have on fluid power and electrical systems?

a] electrical components get damaged in electrical systems

b] fluid power system stops working without damaging the components c] both a] and b]

d] none of the above

192) How is power transmitted in fluid power systems?

a] power is transmitted instantaneously

b] power is transmitted gradually

c] both a] and b]

d] none of the above

193) Generally liquids are non-compressible but when a large pressure of 70 bar is applied, petroleum oil can be compressed up to

a] 0]5% of its original volume

b] 1% of its original volume

c] 5% of its original volume

d] none of the above

194) The resistance offered to the flow of fluid inside a piston develops into

a] pressure

b] force

c] stress

d] all of the above

195) At low pressures, liquids are

a] compressible

b] non-compressible

c] unpredictable

196) In hydraulic systems,

a] the mechanical energy is transferred to the oil and then converted into mechanical energy

b] the electrical energy is transferred to the oil and then converted into mechanical energy

c] the mechanical energy is transferred to the oil and converted into electrical energy

d] none of the above

197) Which of the following is used as a component in hydraulic power unit?

a] pressure gauge

b] filler gauge

c] valve

d] reservoir

198) Rotary motion in a hydraulic power unit is achieved by using

a] hydraulic cylinder
b] pneumatic cylinder
c] both hydraulic and pneumatic cylinder
d] <u>none of the above</u>
199) What is the relation between speed and flow rate for fixed displacement vane pump?
a] <u>flow rate increases with increase in speed of rotor</u>
b] flow rate decreases with increase in speed of rotor
c] flow rate is constant and does not change with change in speed
d] none of the above
200) In fixed displacement vane pump,
a] <u>flow rate decreases with increase in working pressure</u>
b] flow rate increases with increase in working pressure
c] flow rate is constant and does not change with working pressure
d] none of the above
201) Which type of motion is transmitted by hydraulic actuators?
a] linear motion
b] rotary motion
c] <u>both a] and b]</u>
d] none of the above
202) What is the function of electric actuator?
a] <u>converts electrical energy into mechanical torque</u>
b] converts mechanical torque into electrical energy
c] converts mechanical energy into mechanical torque
d] none of the above
203) Which of the following is a hydraulic cylinder based on construction?
a] single acting cylinder
b] double acting cylinder
c] <u>welded design cylinder</u>
d] all of the above
204) Which energy is converted into mechanical energy by the hydraulic cylinders?
a] <u>hydrostatic energy</u>
b] hydrodynamic energy
c] electrical energy
d] none of the above
205) What is the advantage of using a single acting cylinder?

a] high cost and reliable
b] honing inside the inner surface of pump is not required
c] piston seals are not required
d] all of the above
206) What is the function of a flow control valve?
a] flow control valve changes the direction of oil flow
b] flow control valve can adjust the flow rate of hydraulic oil
c] both a] and b]
d] none of the above
207) What does the numbers in 4/2 valve mean?
a] 4 positions and 2 ways
b] 4 ways and 2 positions
c] none of the above
d] 3 ways 2 positions
208) Which type of solenoid has more chances of coil failure?
a] AC solenoid
b] DC solenoid
c] both AC and DC solenoids
d] none of the above
209) Which stage in two stage direction control valve is solenoid operated?
a] main stage direction control valve
b] pilot stage direction control valve
c] both stages in two stage direction control are solenoid operated
d] none of the above
210) Which of the following is a gas charged accumulator?
a] bladder type
b] spring loaded accumulator
c] weighted accumulator
d] all of the above
211) How is pressure of fluid under piston calculated in a weighted accumulator?
a] pressure of fluid = (weight added / piston area)
b] pressure of fluid = (piston area / weight added)
c] pressure of fluid = (weight added / piston force)
d] pressure of fluid = (piston force / weight added)
212) Which of the following gas is used in gas charged accumulator?
a] oxygen

b] <u>nitrogen</u>
c] carbon dioxide
d] all of the above
213) The relation for rapid change in pressure and volume adiabatically is given as
a] p0 v0 = p1 v1 = p2 v2
b] p0 v0 = p1 v1n = p2 v2n
c] <u>p0 v0n = p1 v1n = p2 v2n</u>
d] none of the above
214) Why is the pilot operated check valve used in clamping operation?
a] to reduce leakage in spool valve
b] to avoid decrease in pressure during clamping
c] <u>both a] and b]</u>
d] none of the above
215) Which area does the part shown below indicate?
a] rod area
b] full bore area
c] <u>annulus area</u>
d] none of the above
216) Which of the following statements is true?
a] Meter-in feed circuits have speed control in two directions
b] <u>Standard block feed circuits have speed control in two directions</u>
c] Tank line feed control systems have speed control only in one direction
d] all of the above
217) Leakage in rotary chucks can be compensated by
a] flow control valve
b] pilot operated check valve
c] <u>accumulator</u>
d] all of the above
218) Which valve is used to block the accumulator from the system for the purpose of safety?
a] pilot valve
b] <u>needle valve</u>
c] detent valve
d] all of the above
219) Which of the following systems generate more energy when used in industrial applications?

a] <u>hydraulic systems</u>
b] pneumatic systems
c] both systems generate same energy
d] cannot say
96] For mounting a lathe chuck
A] start it by hand and then turn the power on
B] mount it on by power
C] <u>mount it by hand</u>
D] mount it with the help of a hammer

Lathe Four Jaw Chuck Animation & Video
96] For mounting a lathe chuck
A] start it by hand and then turn the power on
B] mount it on by power
C] <u>mount it by hand</u>
D] mount it with the help of a hammer

Lathe Four Jaw Chuck Animation & Video

158] The following given device which one for used clamping job only?

A] Jig

B] Fixture

C] Housing

D] Gauge

159] While fabricated by welding job which device is used for holding fixed or revolving if necessary up to 360°C of welding job?

A] Gauge

b] Template

C] Jig

D] Fixture

Fixture

160] The main things of drilling jig its not clamping with machine table which reason is correct given following?

A] it is strong for operation

B] it is easy for operation

C] many different size holes produce by different setting while drilling on job

D] for this device has lot of time

161] Following which locations is most usefull for round shape job location?

A] pin type locator

B] wedge type locator

C] vee locator

D] adjustable stop locators

162] Following which reason is correct for using bushing in drilling jigs?

A] easy for drilling

B] for fixed drill hole size

C] for accurate drilling operation

D] for given better finish drilling hole

163] The metal for manufacturing jig bush is...?

A] mild steel

B] cast iron

C] cast steel

D] tool steel

164] Given following bush which busing used for locating renewable bushing?

A] press fit bushing

B] linear bushing
C] special bushing
D] knurd bushing
165] jig has tolerance..?
A] five present of job tolerance
B] ten percent of job tolerance
C] 20% to 50% of job tolerance
D] 100% of job tolerance
166] Following which jig is use for location from bore?
A] plate jig
B] solid jig
C] post jig
D] box jig
167] Following which jig having drill plate?
A] solid jig
B] plate jig
C] box jig
D] table jig
168] Following which locator is used for internal diameter location?
A] solid saports
B] Pin type locator
C] Vee locator
D] nest locator
169] Drm jig bushing-are generally hardened to ------------.
A] Mild steel
B] Cast iron
C] Cast steel
D] Tooi steel
170] Jigs is device which -------------
A] Locate the work piece
B] Holding and supporting the work piece
C] Guide the cutting tool
D] Does all the above
171] Which among the following jigs is used forllocation from a bore?
A] Plate jig
B] Solid jig
C] Post jig
D] Box jig

172] Fixture is a production device which -----------.

A] Holds and locate the work piece

B] Holds the piece

C] Chats the work piece,

D] Neither holds nor. Locates the-work piece

173] Which one of the following is used to guide tool and hold the job in mass production? '

A] Gauge.

B] Housing

C] Fixture

D] Jig

174] Which among the following is the purpose for proi/iding bushing in a drill jig?

A] For locating accurately and guiding the drill for precise drilling operation

B] For determining the size of the hole to be drilled

C] For easy drilling

D] For getting good finished surface in the drilled holes

175] Drill jig are used for? _

A] Drill operations only.

B] Clamping the job for drilling

C] Drilling, Reaming, Tapping and other operations

D] Guiding the tools only

176] Which one of the following jigs consists of drill plate, which rests on the component to be drilled? . . . .

A] Solid jig .

B] Plate jig .

C] Box jig

D] Trunnion jig

177] Jig is a device which -----------

A] Locates the work piece .

B] Hold and supports the work piece and guides tool

C] Guides the cutting tool

D] Hold the cutting tool .

178] Drill jig are used for ....

A] Drilling, reaming, tapping and other allied operations

B] Drilling operations only

C] Clamping the job when drilling

D] Guiding the tool only

179] Fixture is a production device which---------: -----

A] holds the work piece '

B] Locate the work piece

C] Holds and locates the work piece

D] Neither holds nor locates the work piece

180] Purpose of the Box Jig is to

A] Hold the job and guide the tool to produce internal threads

B] To produce many inclined holes

C] To produce many straight holes

D] None of these

181] Jigs and fixtures are --------.

A] Machining tools

B] Precision tools

C] Both (a] & (b]

D] None of these

182] 'How jig are in terms of weight compared to fixtures?

A] Jigs are lighter than fixtures

B] Jigs are heavier than fixtures

C] jigs are equal in weight to fixtures for same operation

D] None of these

183] Which fixtures are used for machining parts which musthav-e machined details evenw spaced?

A] Profile fixtures

B] Duplex fixtures

C] Indexing fixtures

D] None of these

225] Which one of the following is important factor required to achieve the interchange ability in mass production? .

A] Geometrical accuracy.

B] Standardization

C] Dimensional accuracy

D] Surface finish

226] Interchange ability is normally applied for? _

A] Repairing of parts

B] Mass production

C] Single piece production

D] All of these

227] When tolerance given in one side of the basic dimension, it is called ---------

A].Tolerance system

B] Unilateral tolerance

C] Bilateral tolerance

D] Allowance System

228] The measured Size Of the dimensions of a component as called---------

A] Basic size

B] Nominal Size

C] Allowed size

D] Actual size

104] A die in which cutting and non cutting operations are carried out per stroke

A] Piercing die

B] Progressive die

C] Combination die

D] Compound die

105] A die in which two or more sequential operations are performed at two or more stations upon the work

A] Piercing die

B] Progressive die

C] Combination die

D] Compound die

106] A die in which the shape of the punch and die are directly reproduced in the metal with little or no metal flow

A] Progressive die

B] Combination die

C] Compound die

D] Forming die

107] The die used for producing any shape of holes

A] Piercing die

B] Progressive die

C] Combination die

D] Compound die

144]During suction stroke the charge drawn in a petrol engine is

A] air only

B. air and petrol mixture

C] petrol only

D] fuels other than petrol

Petrol engine in car

145] In a petrol engine air fuel mixture is drawn into the cylinder due to vacuum created during

A] power stroke

B] exhaust stroke

C] <u>suction stroke</u>

D] compression stroke

146] the high fuel consumption of a petrol engine may be due to

A] <u>leakage of fuel from carburetor</u>

B] defects in lubrication system

C] air leaks in intake manifold

D] incorrect idle speed (too low)

147] the float circuit is provided in a carburetor

A] to store fuel vapours

B] to supply mixture of air & fuel

C] <u>to maintain proper level of fuel in float chamber</u>

D] none of the above

148] increase or decrease the speed of the engine

B] Speedometer

C] Clutch pedal

D] Ignition switch

E] <u>Accelerator</u>

• 67 •

Engine in vehicle

2] Machine foundation should be separated from adjacent building components by

mean off

A]Flexible joint

B]Expansion joints

C]T-joint

D]Compression joint

Answer- B

3] Which of the following is not a type of foundations for machines
A]Box type
B]Frame type
C]Bare type
D]Block type
Answer- C
4] Which bolt is secure the machine to its foundation
A]Square bolt
B]Eyc bolt
C]T- bolt
D]J-bolt
Answer- D
5 Levelling bolts are used for
A]Rigidity of machine
B]Adjusting the height of machine
C]Supporting the load for machine
D]Adjusting the length of machine
Answer- B
6] Which of the following statement about concrete is correct
A]Can bear both tensile & compressive loads
B]Can not bear both tensile & compressive loading
C]Can bear only tensile load
D]Can not bear tensile load
Answer- D
9] Why free space is kept around the machine
A]For operation only
B]For operation & maintenance
C]For maintenance only
D]For take rest of worker
Answer- B
10] How many types of machine foundation generally used
A]02 types
B]04 types
C]06 types
D]08 types
Answer- B
11] Which type of machine foundation uses a hollow concrete block
A]Frame type

B]Box type

C]Block type

D]Wall type

Answer- B

12] The material of eye foundation bolt is

A]M.S. or W.I.

B]Only M.S.

C]Only W.I.

D]Only Aluminium

Answer- A

13] Which of the following is not machine foundation

A]Block type

B]Wall type

C]Box type

D]Window type

Answer- D

14] What is the shape of lower part of rag bolt

A]Round shape

B]Rectangular shape

C]Triangular shape

D]Pentagonal shape

Answer- B

15] What material Is filled in space around the rag bolt

A]Concrete or sand

B]Oil or water

C]Sulphur or molten lead

D]Cement or sand

Answer- C

16] In which bolt a key is inserted

A]Rag bolt

B]Eye foundation bolt

C]Lewis bolt

D]Square bolt

Answer- C

17] Which type of foundation bolts are used for fixing heavy machines

A]Cotter foundation bolt

B]Eye foundation bolt

C]Rag foundation bolt

D]foundation bolt

Answer- A

18] What is the another name of foundation bolt

A]Nut bolt

B]Anchor bolt

C]Screw bolt

D]Thread bolt

Answer- B

19] Which foundation bolts can be quickly forged from a MS or WI bar

A]Rag foundation bolt

B]Square foundation bolt

C]T Headed foundation bolt

D]Eye foundation bolt

Answer- D

20] In cement grouting what is the mixture of sand & cement

A]4 parts of sand 1 part of cement

B]3 parts of sand 2 part of cement

C]2 parts of sand 1 part of cement

D]1 parts of sand 1 part of cement

Answer- C

21] What is the other name of box type foundation bolt

A]Caisson bolt

B]Ball type bolt

C]Frame type bolt

D]Block type bolt

Answer- A

22] Which of the following is not a foundation bolt

A]Rag bolt

B]Lewis bolt

C]Cotter bolt

D]Nut bolt

Answer- D

23] Which of the following factors ergonomics is related to human for

A]Only comfort

B]Only safety

C]Comfort & safety

D]Hygiene

Answer- C

24] Which of the following is related to ergonomics

A]Terminology

B]Physiology

C]Ophthalmology

D]Anthology

Answer- B

25] The most frequently used components are arranged in which location

A]Left side location

B]Right side location

C]Upper side location

D]Center location

Answer- D

26] Which of the following is used for controlling the rotation more than 360°

A]Knob

B]Crank

C]Wheel

D]Selector

Answer- B

27] How much working area will be covered by the left hand for designing an efficient work

space

A]Normal working area

B]Zero working area

C]Maximum working area

D]Minimum working area

Answer- C

1] What is the full form of CAD

A]Computer Aided Drafting

B]Arrange Drafting

C]Communication Aided Drafting

D]Communication Arrange Drafting

Answer- A

2] What is the default grid spacing in both X & Y direction in AutoCAD

A]20

B]10

C]5

D]15

Answer- B

3] Which of the following is related to the 2D poly line

A]Arc & line together

B]Change the arc to the line

C]Only make arc

D]Change the line to the arc

Answer- A

5] What is the function of insert block in AutoCAD

A]To insert presaved shape in current drawing

B]To open a save shape

C]To save a new shape

D]To edit a new shape

Answer- A

6] Which command is used to cut a line in Auto CAD

A]Extend

B]Trim

C]Delete

D]Offset

Answer- B

7] Which command is used to create specific gap of a line

A]Break two point

B]Break one point

C]Trim

D]Short

Answer- A

8] Which command is used to obtain common region of two intersecting parts in Auto cad

Subtract

Intersect

Revolve

Union

B

9] Which command is used for adding height to 2D figure in Auto cad

A]Extrude

B]Extend

C]Explode

D]Union

Answer- A

10] Which command is use to arrange an object in rectangular matrix or polar grid

A]Copy

B]Move

C]Mirror

D]Array

Answer- D

11 Which type of document can be created to draw in SolidWorks

A]2D document

B]3D document

C]4D document

D]6D document

Answer- B

12] What is the name of drawing when two or more parts joins together

A]Junction

B]Merged

C]Assembly

D]Combination

Answer- C

13] What is called when cutting the corner at an angle

A]Fillet

B]Chamfer

C]Bevel

D]Taper

Answer- B

14] What is the name of outside surface of part in SolidWorks

A]Edge

B]Origin

C]Corner

D]Face

Answer- D

15] What is the function of "cut-extrude feature" in SolidWorks

A]Material removal

B]Material deposition

C]Part removal

D]Part addition

Answer- A

16] Which of the following feature allows the material to a solid in SolidWorks

A]Solid creations mode

B]Feature manager

C]Sketch mode

D]Solid editing mode

Answer- B

17] Which function will create a pocket in a SolidWorks , model

Feature manager

Fillet

Extruded base

Extruded cut

D

18] How it can be changed when once an entity has been defined in SolidWorks

A]Using cut function

B]Changing the input

C]Editing

D]Deleting it

Answer- C

19] Where "Alt F' command is used in SolidWorks

A For file menu

B For zoom in

C For zoom out

D For filter edge " Alt F"

Answer- A

20] Which of the following can be seen first in part option under application option in an invertor

A Sketch on x,y plane

B Sketch on y z plane

C No new sketch

D Sketch on x z plane

Answer- C

21] Which of the following is file extension in inventor

A .Pdf

B .Org

C .drg

D .ipt

Answer- D

22] Which one is not seen in "draw tool bar" in invertor

A Circle

B Rectangle

C Axis

D Arc

Answer- C

23] Which command is not seen in surface option in model tool bar in an invertor

A Stitch

B Thicken

C Sculpt

D Axis

Answer- D

24] In which tool bar the free orbit tool is found in 3D modelling

A Rotate

B Modify

C Move

D 3D move

Answer- B

25] By which feature a cylinder can be created by drawing a rectangular shape

A Revolve

B Move

C Extrude

D Sweep

Answer- A

26] By which all the part drawing can be made visible in the graphic area

A Sketch tool bar

B Selection filter

C Command manager

D Property manager

Answer- B

27] Towards which side in the view tool bar will position the view of the 3D solid

A SE Isometric

B Right EW

C Isometric

D Front

Answer- A

1] What is defined by the sheet format dialogue box for creating drawing sheet in solid works

A Sheet format only

B Paper size only

C Sheet format & paper size

D Feature managar

Answer- C

2] Which one of the following is the default standard sheet format A -Landscape.slddrt

to create drawing sheet in solid woorks

A I. S. default

B A. S. default

C B.A. default

D U.S. default

Answer- D

3] Which one path is used to add drawing items in solid works

A Insert > model items

B Insert > angle view

C Insert > name view

D Insert > add view

Answer- A

4] Which icon is used to open named view dialogue box in solid works

A ANew edit icon

B New add icon

C New view icon

D New open icon

Answer- C

5] Where the view pallete opens to generate standard 3 views in solid works

A Right side of the window

B Left side of the window

C Top side of the window

D Bottom side of the window

Answer- A

7] Which one of the following is similar to an
auxiliary view generally in solid works

A Angle view

B Projected view

C Named view

D Standard view

Answer- B

8] Which of the following line is used to create

sectional view of an object in solid works

A Cutting plane line

B Ditto line

C Phantom line

D Section line

Answer- D

9] Which view in general is used to create a new drawing view which is enlarged portion

of existing view

A Named view

B Three view

C Sectional view

D Detail view

Answer- D

10] Which of the following is used to create exploded views in solid works

A Configuration manager

B Show preview

C Show tree items

D Collapse itmes

Answer- A

11] Which command is used to create animations based on mates

A Movable contrille

B Rigid controller

C Mate controller

D Fix controller

Answer- C

12] Which of the following is a mate used in animation controller

A DIAMETER

B ANGLE

C LENGTH

D RADIUS

Answer- C

14] Which command contains the diameter symbol, and the dimension of the hole

diameter

A Radius out

B Demension out

C Dia out

D Call out

Answer- D

15] Which annotation tool is used to select the location for the first leader as well as many

additional leaders

A Note

B Point

C First

D Section

Answer- A

16] Where simulation name appears in solid works

A Tittle bar

B Menu bar

C View bar

D Tool bar

Answer- B

17] Which one of the following is not file extension for solid works

A .slljpg

B .sldprt

C .sldasm

D .slddrw

Answer- A

18 Which of the following is useful in drawing orthographic views in solid works

A Dashed line cosmetic threads

B Shaded cosmetic threads

C Template threads

D Linear threads

Answer- B

1 Which of the following is used to assign the material to a solid in solid works

A Feature manager

B Sketch mode

C Solid creation

D Solid work

Answer- A

2 Which is a computer added design tool or software that runs on MS-Window

A Tally

B Coral Draw

C Solid works

D Page maker

Answer- C

3 Which of the following is used to assemble two parts with each other

A Mate property manager

B Manager property manager

C Move property manager

D Confiuration property manager

Answer- A

4 Where is design tree in the solid works located

A Top from property manager

B Below from property manager

C Left to property manager

D Right to Property manager

Answer- B

5 Which solid works certification is popular

A CACP

B CSWP

C CACA

D CSWPP

Answer- B

6 Where is the command manager in solid works located

A Left of graphic area

B Right of graphic area

C Top of graphic area

D Bottom of graphic area

Answer- A

7 Which short cut key is used to open a doccument in solid works

A Ctrl + P

B Ctrl + R

C Ctrl + S

D Ctrl + O

Answer- D

8 Which command is used to provide bevel shape of edges in solid works

A Chamfer

B Fillet

C Cut

D Revolve

Answer- B

9 Which of the following is not included in inside build check tools of solid works

A Document checks

B Animation checks

C Dimension check

D Detailed document check

Answer- D

10 What do you understand by a template in solid works

A To open default setting

B To create default setting

C To save default setting

D To edit default setting

Answer- A

11 What is the window that shows you a thumbnail view of the whole e-drawing

A Over view window

B Under view window

C Upper view window

D Lower view window

Answer- A

12 How do you create an e-drawing

A Click open

B Click create

C Click publish

D Click edit

Answer- C

13 What action does the home command performed

A Selection of default view

B Enlarging the default view
C Reducing the default view
D Return to default view
Answer- D
14 Which command performes a non stop replay of drawing animation
A Continuous play
B Non Continuous play
C Increase play
D Decrease play
Answer- A
15 What visual aid helps you to identify model onientation in drawing
A 3D pointer
B 2D pointer
C 4D pointer
D 6D pointer
Answer- A
16 Which one of the following is not for inserting a reference plane
A Go to insert > ref.geo > plane
B Go to insert > ref.geo > line
C Go to insert > ref.geo > points
D Go to insert > ref.geo > circle
Answer- D
17 Which of the following is the type of pattern in solid works assembly
A Mirror
B Linear component pattern
C Circular component pattern
D Ractangular component pattern
Answer- D

www.ingramcontent.com/pod-product-compliance
Lightning Source LLC
Chambersburg PA
CBHW050756160726
48004CB00002B/588